Soap

Soapmaking 101: Beginning Cold Process Soapmaking

Soapmaking Studio Class Workbook

Student Edition

Kerri Mixon

Acute Publications
Spring Valley

Kerri Mixon is a 16th generation soapmaker and the owner of multiple soap-related businesses. Her articles on soapmaking have appeared in numerous trade publications. A seasoned instructor, she has taught soapmaking classes to students and live audiences across the United States. Master soapmaker Kerri Mixon's passion for soapmaking is obviously contagious; several graduates of her soapmaking classes now run their own successful soap, body care, and cosmetics businesses.

More Soapmaking Studio Class Workbooks by Kerri Mixon
Soapmaking 101: Beginning Cold Process Soapmaking (Student Edition)
Soapmaking 101: Beginning Cold Process Soapmaking (Teacher Edition)
Soapmaking 105: Intermediate Hot Process Soapmaking
Soapmaking 210: Advanced Cold/Hot Process Soapmaking
Soapmaking 214: Intermediate Transparent Bar Soapmaking
Soapmaking 215: Intermediate Liquid Soapmaking
Soapmaking 220: Coloring and Scenting Soap
Soap Garden 224: Cultivating, Drying, and Adding Herbs to Soap
Soapmaking 225: Water Substitution in Soapmaking
Soap Business 320: Forming a Legal Business Entity to Sell Soap
Soap Business 330: Soap Labeling and Marketing
Soap Business 335: Shrink Wrapping Soap
Soap Business 340: Packaging and Shipping Soap Worldwide
Soap Business 350: Website Design and Internet Commerce
Limited Edition Publication: Bath Bombs, Bath Fizzies, and Bath Salts
Limited Edition Publication: Aromatherapy Natural Perfumes

Soapmaking 101: Beginning Cold Process Soapmaking
Soapmaking Studio Class Workbook
By Kerri Mixon

Acute Publications, Spring Valley 91976
© 2013 by Kerri Mixon
All rights reserved. Published 2013.
Printed in the United States of America.

ISBN-13: 978-0-615-83394-1
ISBN-10: 0-615-83394-2

Cover photographs by Rita Mixon.

Dedication

This book is dedicated to soapmaker and friend Connie DiPronio, who fiercely encouraged me to open a soapmaking school. It is also dedicated to my parents and my wonderful husband David Perez, who undertook numerous unusual chores in order to give me time to write. Finally, it is dedicated to the readers who will carefully strive to be responsible soapmakers.

Narrator: *What are we doing tonight?*
Tyler Durden: *Tonight? We make soap.*
(Fight Club 1999)

Contents

Preface   ix

Acknowledgments   xi

Introduction   xiii

1   Using Lye to Make Soap   1

2   Lye Safety and Protective Equipment   3

3   MSDS for Sodium Hydroxide, Solid (Lye)   9

4   Choosing a Scale   15

5   Choosing a Soap Mold   16

6   Creating the Soap Recipe   17

7   Oil Specification Sheets   19

8   Understanding Saponification Values   21

9   Chart of Saponification Values   22

10   Lye Discount or Oil Superfat   25

11   Calculating the Water   26

12   The Class Soap Recipe   27

13   Make Your Own Soap at Home   28

Notes   30

Bookstore   37

Vendors   39

Registration Form   41

Glossary   43

Index   47

Preface

In the early part of this century, I established public luncheons open to soapmakers in my local southern California area because I was hungry for the company of kindred spirits. To entice other soapmakers to attend, I invited guest speakers such as vegetable oil distributors, fragrance oil manufacturers, successful small business entrepreneurs, and marketing development professionals. Many of the speakers were experts in their fields but could not relate their subject matter directly to home soap manufacture and I was asked to interpose with the specific relevance of some of the topics. For example, the vegetable oil distributors knew all about coconut oil and how it was extracted and refined but they had no idea it attributed to a quick abundant but short-lived lather in soap. During each luncheon the attendees craved these significant connections to soapmaking and I frequently spoke to interject with associations to soapmaking.

As we soapmakers continued to meet four times per year at the SoCal Soapmakers' Luncheons, more and more luncheon attendees requested I hold private soapmaking lessons from my home. I was against the idea from the beginning and I felt being responsible for the public at large coming to my home to work with caustic lye could only end in disaster. My husband David encouraged me to go out on a limb to help fellow soapmakers, so I researched and considered the idea of a soapmaking school for more than a year. After hours spent on the phone to my insurance company, city officials, and the fire marshal, I decided to open the Soapmaking Studio to help others learn the craft for which I have endless passion.

I successfully taught the Soapmaking 101: Beginning Cold Process Soapmaking class for many years using this text and finally decided it should be available to the public to help other soapmaking teachers in their soapmaking schools. This workbook is available in both student and teacher editions, to help others with their endeavors to learn and teach the art of making soap. I still own several soapmaking companies and the soapmaking school and don't plan to retire any time soon. I continue to host the SoCal Soapmakers' Luncheons and "eat, sleep, and breathe soapmaking."

Acknowledgments

I (Kerri Mixon) wrote much of the information in chapters 1, 3, and 10 for Certified Lye in 2006. Certified Lye holds the copyright for the information, which appears on the website http://www.certified-lye.com. The material is reprinted with permission from Certified Lye.

The avocado oil specification sheet on page 19 was created by Cibaria Soap Supply (an oil distributor in Riverside, California) and is reprinted with permission from Karen Moore.

The avocado oil specification sheet on page 20 was generated by Natural Oils International (an oil distributor in Simi Valley, California) and is reprinted with permission from Barbara Hardy.

Many of the companies listed in the "Vendors" section (on page 39) have helped me along the path to soapmaking enlightenment.

Introduction

This Soapmaking Studio Class Workbook, Soapmaking 101: Beginning Cold Process Soapmaking, and the companion soapmaking class explain why online soap recipes and book recipes do not list the correct amounts of sodium hydroxide and may result in lye-heavy soap. This workbook and the class contain vital soapmaking information regarding saponification values and the importance of using saponification values to calculate soap recipes.

The text includes a formula for calculating how much soap to make in order to fill a soap mold. With this capability, a soapmaker need not worry about where to put caustic extra soap batter when too much soap is made, nor worry about not producing enough soap and having short bars of soap.

This workbook also includes formulations to complete the saponification process in the mold (without heat), so no lye is present in the soap when it is removed from the mold, thus doing away with the practice of curing soap bars on a shelf for six weeks.

After completing the workbook and the class, students will be able to safely and confidently make soap by hand in their own homes. Many graduates of Soapmaking 101 now appreciate the skills involved in successful home soapmaking. Creating soap with one's own oils, scents, colors, and herbs is both rewarding and addictive.

This workbook is not a standalone book to learn the art of soapmaking. It is a companion product to the Soapmaking 101: Beginning Cold Process Soapmaking class offered at the Soapmaking Studio in Lemon Grove, California. Through internet video conferencing the class is also offered as an online eClass from the www.SoapmakingStudio.com website.

Because this workbook is published in both a student edition and a teacher edition, the Soapmaking 101: Beginning Cold Process Soapmaking class will become available at other soapmaking schools and more locations across the county.

Chapter 1
Using Lye to Make Soap

Soap is defined as the salt of a fatty acid. Without sodium hydroxide, there can be no soap. When soap is made correctly, there is no sodium hydroxide present in the finished soap. Water is needed to dissolve the sodium hydroxide. Fats, such as vegetable oils, provide the fatty acids. This workbook focuses on the cold process method of making soap because no heat is needed to complete the saponification reaction. Although, saturated fats solid at room temperature (such as coconut oil or palm oil) must first be warmed to liquefy them in order to thoroughly mix them into the soap.

Lye + **Water** + **Fat**

= **Soap**

Saponification

Saponification is the chemical process of making soap that involves an exothermic reaction between lye (sodium hydroxide) and a fat (usually oils). What is commonly known as cold process soapmaking yields a glycerin-rich soap, which used to be referred to as "lye soap." People often think of lye soap as a soap that is unpleasant to use because too much lye was used in the soap formula and lye (sodium hydroxide) remained in the bar of soap to irritate and burn the skin. Soap cannot be made without using lye. When made correctly, no lye will remain in the bar of soap.

Historic "Lye Soap"

Throughout history, soap was made by rendering available animal fats and adding natural lye (leached from hardwood ashes) to make soap. Without the scientific data readily available today, the soapmakers of yesteryear approximated the amount of lye to add to the fats. If not enough lye was added, with too many fats remaining, the mixture would separate, not be useable, and the effort and time of preparation would be wasted. If too much lye was added, some extra lye would remain in the soap but the soap could be used. Therefore, the preference was to add extra lye to ensure the soap would be useable. However, the extra lye remaining in the bar of soap made it unpleasant to use because it would often irritate or burn the skin.

Saponification Value

Today, with easy access to the exact composition of a fat and the molecular weight of a fat, it is easy to determine the exact amount of lye needed to completely saponify a measured amount of a specific fat, so there will not be any extra lye in the soap and the soap will not irritate the skin.

The number of milligrams of potassium hydroxide required to completely saponify one gram of a specific fat is referred to as the "saponification value." Note: Laboratories usually refer to the saponification value of potassium hydroxide, not sodium hydroxide.

Potassium hydroxide is commonly used to make liquid soap and sodium hydroxide is necessary for making solid bars of soap. The numbers in the chart of saponification values, on page 22, are listed for lye (sodium hydroxide) and have been converted from potassium hydroxide to sodium hydroxide and from milligrams to be generically applicable to any consistent unit of weight.

(See "Chart of Saponification Values" on page 22.)

The transformation of raw soap batter into solid soap as the lye continues to completely react with the fat is called "saponification completion." Depending upon the formulation of ingredients and the type of soapmaking process, the saponification reaction may complete in the soap pot, in the mold, or on the curing rack.

> **The successful completion of saponification depends upon utilizing 1 of 3 factors: Time** (waiting 6 weeks), **Heat** (hot process method), **or Water** (formula on page 26).

Chapter 2
Lye Safety and Protective Equipment

First Aid

Danger-Poison! Corrosive: Causes eye damage and severe skin burns!

If swallowed:
> Rinse mouth with water and drink one or two glasses of water. Do not induce vomiting! Immediately get medical attention or call your poison control center at 1-800-222-1222.

If in eyes:
> Immediately flush eyes with water. Remove any contact lenses and continue to flush eyes with water for at least 20 minutes. Immediately get medical attention or call your poison control center at 1-800-222-1222.

If on skin:
> Gently wipe product from skin and remove any contaminated clothing. Flush skin with plenty of water for at least 15 minutes and then wash thoroughly with soap and water. Contact a physician or call your poison control center at 1-800-222-1222.

Do NOT Allow Vinegar to Contact Lye!

High school chemistry students are taught never to mix acids with bases. Vinegar is an acid solution consisting of 5% acetic acid in water and as a pH of 3. Sodium hydroxide is a strong base with a pH of 14. The two should never be combined. Never use vinegar to clean a lye spill. All MSDS for sodium hydroxide specify lye spills should only be cleaned with plain water.

Safety

Solid sodium hydroxide and solutions containing high concentrations of sodium hydroxide may cause chemical burns, permanent injury or scarring, and blindness. Lye (sodium hydroxide) may be harmful or fatal if swallowed.

Solvation of sodium hydroxide is highly exothermic, and the resulting heat may cause heat burns or ignite flammables (such as liquid fragrances).

Avoid all contact with organic tissue (including human skin, eyes, mouth, and animals or pets). Keep away from clothing. Avoid all contact with aluminum.

The combination of aluminum and sodium hydroxide results in a large production of hydrogen gas: $2Al(s) + 6NaOH(aq) \rightarrow 3H_2(g) + 2Na_3AlO_3(aq)$. Hydrogen gas is explosive; mixing lye (sodium hydroxide) and aluminum in a closed container is therefore dangerous. In addition to aluminum, lye (sodium hydroxide) may also react with magnesium, zinc (galvanized), tin, chromium, brass, and bronze to produce hydrogen gas and is therefore dangerous. Do not allow lye (sodium hydroxide) to contact these metals.

Lye (sodium hydroxide) may react with various sugars to generate carbon monoxide, which is a poisonous gas; mixing sodium hydroxide and sugar in a closed container is therefore dangerous. Do not allow lye to contact sugar or honey, except outdoors.

Personal Protection

Personal protection for the safe handling of lye (sodium hydroxide) includes safety glasses, chemical-resistant gloves, and adequate ventilation. When in the close proximity of lye (sodium hydroxide) dissolving in an open container of water, a vapor-resistant facemask is recommended. Certified Lye sells these personal protection items (and more).

Storage

Lye (sodium hydroxide) is a deliquescent salt and has a strong affinity for moisture. Lye will deliquesce (dissolve or melt) when exposed to open air. Sodium hydroxide will absorb a relatively large amount of water from the atmosphere (air) if exposed to it. Eventually, it will absorb enough water to form a liquid solution because it will dissolve in the water it absorbs. Lye (sodium hydroxide) should be stored in an airtight re-sealable container.

Hygroscopic substances (such as packets of silica gel) are often used as desiccants to draw moisture away from water-sensitive items. Desiccants should never be placed inside a canister of lye (sodium hydroxide) because lye is also hygroscopic and has much stronger hygroscopic properties than activated carbon and silica gel (the most common ingredients in commercial desiccant packets). Lye will pull and absorb the water from the desiccant packets and eventually melt or dissolve from the moisture introduced into the canister by the desiccant packets. Do not place desiccant packets inside containers of lye (sodium hydroxide).

Lye should be stored in airtight plastic containers made of HDPE. It is recommended the containers for storing lye have a square perimeter; a cylindrical container accidentally knocked on its side may roll and continue to spill lye along its path of travel. The containers should be labeled to indicate the potential danger of the contents and stored away from children, pets, acids, and moisture. Certified Lye sells 4" by 4" Hazard Class 8 corrosive material warning label stickers.

For more information on lye safety, consult an MSDS for lye (sodium hydroxide). (MSDS for lye is on page 9.)

Lye Quality

Commercial or industrial grade lye is commonly used as oven cleaner or drain opener and is an inferior grade of lye that may contain contaminants (such as large amounts of sodium carbonate). Commercial or industrial grade lye is not suitable for making soap.

Food grade lye is affordable and is preferred for soapmaking.

The cost of laboratory or technical grade lye is cost prohibitive. Stored and used under a vacuum, laboratory or technical grade lye is extremely expensive. Once exposed to air (if not opened under a vacuum) laboratory grade lye becomes food grade lye.

Eye Protection for Soapmakers

One granule of sodium hydroxide or one drop of lye solution in an eye can cause blindness. Spare no expense when protecting eyes. Soap batter, no matter how tick or thin, is corrosive enough to cause eye damage. The following safety glasses are available from Certified Lye and the Soapmaking Studio.

Modern Safety Glasses

Modern safety glasses are shatter-resistant with anti-fog lenses and meet the stricter ANSI (Z87.1) safety standard. Comfortable earpieces do not hook around ear and never need adjusting; specially designed rubber earpieces provide a secure fit, so one size fits all. The stylish clear rim offers a modern look and features wraparound side shields to provide complete protection. Remember: Safety glasses are a must! Just one drop of lye solution in an eye can cause blindness.

Traditional Safety Glasses

Traditional style plastic safety glasses are shatter-resistant with anti-fog lenses and meet the stricter ANSI (Z87.1) safety standard. Length of earpieces is fully adjustable, so one size fits all. Wraparound side shields provide complete protection. Remember: Safety glasses are a must! Just one drop of lye solution in an eye can cause blindness.

Universal Safety Glasses

Wear these universal safety glasses over prescription eyeglasses or alone. Universal safety glasses meet the stricter ANSI (Z87.1) safety standard and feature top and side shields to provide complete protection. Remember: Safety glasses are a must! Just one drop of lye solution in an eye can cause blindness.

UV Outdoor Safety Sunglasses

UV outdoor safety sunglasses feature a wraparound style, offer UV protection, and meet the stricter ANSI (Z87.1) safety standard. Comfortable earpieces do not hook around ear and never need adjusting, so one size fits all. These safety sunglasses are great for soap makers who avoid harmful lye vapors by mixing their lye water outdoors. Remember: Safety glasses are a must! Just one drop of lye solution in an eye can cause blindness.

NFPA 704 Diamond Placard for Lye (Sodium Hydroxide)

This image is the NFPA 704 diamond placard for lye (sodium hydroxide).

NFPA 704 Rating Definitions

Blue (left):
> Health rating 3: Short exposure could cause serious temporary or residual injury.

Red (top):
> Flammability rating 0: Will not burn.

Yellow (right):
> Reactivity rating 1: Normally stable, but can become unstable at elevated temperatures and pressures.

White (bottom):
> Special symbol COR: Corrosive.

Transporting Lye

Warning! It is illegal to ship lye without a certified DOT number, without meeting very strict shipping criteria, and without having passed an annual certified Hazmat shipper exam. Do not attempt to ship lye! (Not even a little bit. Not on eBay. Not through the mail. Not through UPS. Nothing!) **It will not be worth the fine if you are caught or if someone is injured.**

It is also illegal to transport lye on an airplane as a passenger or in checked luggage. Do not take lye on an airplane.

It is legal to transport a small canister of lye in your personal vehicle and to store it in your home. Driving with 200 pounds of lye or any amount over 200 pounds requires Hazmat registration with the US Department of Transportation.

If planning to visit an out-of-state friend to share the experience of making soap, order a small amount of lye from a legal lye distributor and have the lye delivered to the friend's home.

Lye General Specifications

This is the universal diamond placard for Class 8 hazardous materials, such as lye (sodium hydroxide). The Hazard Class of 8 indicates a corrosive material. Certified Lye sells 4" by 4" Hazard Class 8 corrosive material warning label stickers.

Lye (Sodium Hydroxide)
- Proper Shipping Name: Sodium hydroxide, solid
- Hazard Class: 8 (Corrosive)
- Identification Number: UN1823
- Packing Group: II
- CAS Registry Number: 1310-73-2
- Molecular Formula: NaOH
- Molecular Mass: 39.9971 g/mol
- Density and Phase: 2.1 g/cm³, solid
- Solubility in Water: 111 g/100 ml (20 °C)
- Melting Point: 318 °C (591 K)
- Boiling Point: 1390 °C (1663 K)
- Flash Point: Not applicable; not flammable
- Basicity (pKb): -2.43
- pH: 14 (5% aq soln)
- EPA Toxicity Class: I (Danger-Poison! Corrosive—causes eye damage and severe skin burns)
- Risk Phrases: R22 (harmful if swallowed), R35 (causes severe burns)
- Safety Phrases: S1 (keep locked up), S2 (keep out of the reach of children), S26 (in case of contact with eyes, rinse immediately with plenty of water and seek medical advice), S36 (wear suitable protective clothing), S37 (wear suitable gloves), S39 (wear eye/face protection), S45 (in case of accident or if you feel unwell seek medical advice immediately; show the label where possible)
- Synonyms: Lye, caustic soda, sodium hydrate, white caustic, soda lye, soda ash, ascarite

For more information on sodium hydroxide and lye safety, consult the MSDS for lye in chapter 3. The MSDS for lye (on page 9) is provided by Certified Lye.

To promote the safe handling and safe storage of sodium hydroxide, Certified Lye has given permission for all soapmaking students, graduates, and guest soapmakers to reproduce the MSDS for lye from chapter 3.

If you have any employees (including yourself) who contact a hazardous material, such as lye, you are required by law to keep an updated MSDS on file. The MSDS is to be stored near the location of the lye, not with the final soap. If a soapmaker goes to sell soap at a craft fair, the soapmaker need not bring the MSDS to the craft fair because only the final soap is present at the craft fair; the lye is not located at the craft fair.

Chapter 3
MSDS for Sodium Hydroxide, Solid (Lye)

Section 1 - Chemical Product and Company Identification

MSDS Name: Sodium hydroxide, solid.
Synonyms: Lye, sodium hydrate, white caustic, caustic soda, soda lye, soda ash, ascarite.
Company Identification:
Certified Lye
PO Box 133
Spring Valley, CA 91976-0133
Website: http://www.certified-lye.com
Email: info@certified-lye.com
Telephone: 619-548-2378
Poison Control Center: 800-222-1222
Chemtrec: 800-424-9300

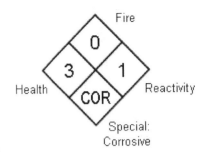

Section 2 - Composition, Information on Ingredients

CAS#, Chemical Name, Percent, EINECS/ELINCS:
1310-73-2, Sodium hydroxide, 99-100, 215-185-5.
497-19-8, Sodium carbonate, <1.0, 207-838-8.
Food Chemical Codex (FCC):
These chemicals meet the FDA requirements for food use.

Section 3 - Hazards Identification

Emergency Overview
Appearance: White solid.
Danger! Causes eye and skin burns. Causes digestive and respiratory tract burns. Hygroscopic (absorbs moisture from the air).
Target Organs: Eyes, skin, mucous membranes.
Potential Health Effects
Eye: Causes eye burns. May cause blindness. May cause chemical conjunctivitis and corneal damage.
Skin: Causes skin burns. May cause deep, penetrating ulcers of the skin.
Ingestion: May cause severe and permanent damage to the digestive tract. Causes gastrointestinal tract burns. May cause perforation of the digestive tract. Causes severe pain, nausea, vomiting, diarrhea, and shock.
Inhalation: Irritation may lead to chemical pneumonitis and pulmonary edema. Causes severe irritation of upper respiratory tract with coughing, burns, breathing difficulty, and possible coma. Causes chemical burns to the respiratory tract.
Chronic: Prolonged or repeated skin contact may cause dermatitis. Effects may be delayed.

Section 4 - First Aid Measures

Eyes: In case of contact, immediately flush eyes with plenty of water for a t least 15 minutes. Get medical aid immediately.
Skin: In case of contact, immediately flush skin with plenty of water for at least 15 minutes. Immediately remove contaminated clothing and shoes. Get medical aid immediately. Wash clothing before reuse.
Ingestion: If swallowed, do NOT induce vomiting. Get medical aid immediately. If victim is fully conscious, give a cupful of water. Never give anything by mouth to an unconscious person.
Inhalation: If inhaled, remove to fresh air. If not breathing, give artificial respiration. If breathing is difficult, give oxygen. Get medical aid.
Notes to Physician: Treat symptomatically and supportively.

Section 5 - Fire Fighting Measures

General Information: As in any fire, wear a self-contained breathing apparatus in pressure-demand, MSHA/NIOSH (approved or equivalent), and full protective gear. Use water spray to keep fire-exposed containers cool. Use water with caution and in flooding amounts. Contact with moisture or water may generate sufficient heat to ignite nearby combustible materials. Contact with metals may evolve flammable hydrogen gas.

Extinguishing Media: Substance is noncombustible; use agent most appropriate to extinguish surrounding fire. Do not get water inside containers.

Flammability: Nonflammable.

Flash Point: Not applicable.

Autoignition Temperature: Not applicable.

Flammable Limits: Not available.

NFPA Rating: Health: 3; Flammability: 0; Instability: 1.

Section 6 - Accidental Release Measures

General Information: Use proper personal protective equipment as indicated in Section 8.

Spills/Leaks: Vacuum or sweep up material and place into a suitable disposal container. Avoid runoff into storm sewers and ditches that lead to waterways. Clean up spills immediately, observing precautions in the Protective Equipment section. Avoid generating dusty conditions. Provide ventilation. Do not get water on spilled substances or inside containers.

Section 7 - Handling and Storage

Handling: Wash thoroughly after handling. Do not allow water to get into the container because of violent reaction. Minimize dust generation and accumulation. Do not get in eyes, on skin, or on clothing. Keep container tightly closed. Avoid ingestion and inhalation. Discard contaminated shoes. Use only with adequate ventilation.

Storage: Store in a tightly closed container. Store in a cool, dry, well-ventilated area away from incompatible substances. Keep away from metals. Keep away from acids. Store protected from moisture. Containers must be tightly closed to prevent the conversion of NaOH to sodium carbonate by the CO_2 in air.

Section 8 - Exposure Controls, Personal Protection

Engineering Controls: Facilities storing or utilizing this material should be equipped with an eyewash facility and a safety shower. Use adequate general or local exhaust ventilation to keep airborne concentrations below the permissible exposure limits.

Exposure Limits

Chemical Name, ACGIH (TLV), NIOSH (REL), OSHA (PEL):

Sodium hydroxide, 2 mg/m^3 Ceiling, 10 mg/m^3 Ceiling (15 minutes), 2 mg/m^3 TWA.

Sodium carbonate, none listed, none listed, none listed.

NIOSH IDLH Concentration: 10 mg/m^3.

OSHA Vacated PEL: None of these chemicals have an OSHA Vacated PEL.

Personal Protective Equipment

Eyes: Wear chemical splash goggles or ANSI-rated safety glasses and face shield.

Skin: Wear gloves, apron, and/or clothing made of butyl rubber, nitrile rubber, and/or polyethylene.

Clothing: Wear appropriate protective clothing to prevent skin exposure.

Respirator: A respiratory protection program that meets OSHA's 29 CFR 1910.134 and ANSI Z88.2 requirements or European Standard EN 149 must be followed whenever workplace conditions warrant respirator use.

Section 9 - Physical and Chemical Properties

Physical State: Solid.
Appearance: White pellets.
Odor: Odorless.
pH: 14 (5% aq soln).
Vapor Pressure: 1 mm Hg @ 739 deg C.
Vapor Density: Not available.
Evaporation Rate: Not available.
Viscosity: Not available.
Boiling Point: 1390 deg C @ 760 mm Hg.
Freezing/Melting Point: 318 deg C.
Decomposition Temperature: Not available.
Solubility: Soluble.
Specific Gravity/Density: 2.13 g/cm^3.
Molecular Formula: NaOH.
Molecular Weight: 40.00.

Section 10 - Stability and Reactivity

Chemical Stability: Stable at room temperature in closed containers under normal storage and handling conditions.
Conditions to Avoid: Moisture, contact with water, exposure to moist air or water, prolonged exposure to air.
Incompatibilities with Other Materials: Water, metals, acids, aluminum, zinc, tin, nitromethane, leather, flammable liquids, organic halogens, wool.
Hazardous Decomposition Products: Toxic fumes of sodium oxide.
Hazardous Polymerization: Will not occur.

Section 11 - Toxicological Information

NIOSH RTECS#
CAS# 1310-73-2 (sodium hydroxide): WB4900000
CAS# 497-19-8 (sodium carbonate): VZ4050000

LD50/
LC50
CAS# 1310-73-2:
Draize test, rabbit, eye: 400 ug Mild;
Draize test, rabbit, eye: 1% Severe;
Draize test, rabbit, eye: 50 ug/24H Severe;
Draize test, rabbit, eye: 1 mg/24H Severe;
Draize test, rabbit, skin: 500 mg/24H Severe.

CAS# 497-19-8:
Draize test, rabbit, eye: 100 mg/24H Moder;
Draize test, rabbit, eye: 50 mg Severe;
Draize test, rabbit, skin: 500 mg/24H Mild;
Inhalation, mouse: LC50 = 1200 mg/m^3/2H;
Inhalation, rat: LC50 = 2300 mg/m^3/2H;
Oral, mouse: LD50 = 6600 mg/kg;
Oral, mouse: LD50 = 6600 mg/kg;
Oral, rat: LD50 = 4090 mg/kg.

Carcinogenicity
CAS# 1310-73-2: Not listed by ACGIH, IARC, NTP, or CA Prop 65.
CAS# 497-19-8: Not listed by ACGIH, IARC, NTP, or CA Prop 65.
Epidemiology: No information found.
Teratogenicity: No information found.
Reproductive Effects: No information found.
Mutagenicity: See actual entry in RTECS for complete information.
Neurotoxicity: No information found.

Section 12 - Ecological Information

No information available.

Section 13 - Disposal Considerations

Chemical waste generators must determine whether a discarded chemical is classified as a hazardous waste. US EPA guidelines for the classification determination are listed in 40 CFR 261.3. Additionally, waste generators must consult state and local hazardous waste regulations to ensure complete and accurate classification.

RCRA F List: None of these chemicals are listed in 40 CFR 261.31.
RCRA K List: None of these chemicals are listed in 40 CFR 261.32.
RCRA P List: None of these chemicals are listed in 40 CFR 261.33(e).
RCRA U List: None of these chemicals are listed in 40 CFR 261.33(f).

Section 14 - Transport Information

US DOT, Canada TDG
Shipping Name: Sodium hydroxide, solid; Sodium hydroxide, solid.
Hazard Class: 8, 8.
UN Number: UN1823, UN1823.
Packing Group: II, II.

Section 15 - Regulatory Information

US Federal Regulations
TSCA Section 8(b):
CAS# 1310-73-2 is listed on the TSCA inventory.
CAS# 497-19-8 is listed on the TSCA inventory.
TSCA Section 12(b): None of these chemicals are listed under TSCA Section 12(b).
TSCA Significant New Use Rule: None of these chemicals have a TSCA SNUR.
Chemical Test Rules: None of these chemicals have a Chemical Test Rule.
Health & Safety Reporting List:
None of these chemicals are on the Health & Safety Reporting List.
SARA Title III/EPCRA:
None of these chemicals have a TPQ under EPCRA Section 302 (EHS).
None of these chemicals are reportable under EPCRA Section 304.
None of these chemicals are reportable under EPCRA Section 313.
SARA Codes:
CAS# 1310-73-2: Immediate, reactive.
CAS# 497-19-8: Immediate.
CERCLA Hazardous Substances and Corresponding RQ:
CAS# 1310-73-2: 1000 lb final RQ; 454 kg final RQ.
CAS# 497-19-8: This chemical is not listed and has no RQ.
Clean Air Act:
None of these chemicals are listed under CAA Section 112(r).
None of these chemicals are listed as hazardous air pollutants.
None of these chemicals are listed as Class 1 or Class 2 Ozone Depletors.
Clean Water Act:
CAS# 1310-73-2 is listed as a Hazardous Substance under the CWA Section 311.
None of these chemicals are listed as Priority Pollutants under the CWA Section 303.
None of these chemicals are listed as Toxic Pollutants under the CWA Section 307.
OSHA: None of these chemicals are considered highly hazardous by OSHA.
SARA Title III/EPCRA States' Right-To-Know Lists:
CAS# 1310-73-2 is listed by California, Massachusetts, Minnesota, New Jersey, and Pennsylvania.
CAS# 497-19-8 is not listed by CA, FL, MA, MN, NJ, or PA.
California Prop 65:
None of these chemicals are listed on the California Carcinogenic Chemicals list.

European/International Regulations
European Labeling in Accordance with EC Directives
Hazard Symbols: C.

Risk Phrases:

R 22 (harmful if swallowed),

R 35 (causes severe burns).

Safety Phrases:

S1 (keep locked up),

S2 (keep out of the reach of children),

S26 (in case of contact with eyes, rinse immediately with plenty of water and seek medical advice),

S36 (wear suitable protective clothing),

S37 (wear suitable gloves),

S39 (wear eye/face protection),

S45 (in case of accident or if you feel unwell, seek medical advice immediately; show the label where possible).

WGK (Water Danger/Protection):
CAS# 1310-73-2: 1.

CAS# 497-19-8: 1.

Canada – DSL/NDSL:
CAS# 1310-73-2 is listed on Canada's Domestic Substances List.

CAS# 497-19-8 is listed on Canada's Domestic Substances List.

Canada – WHMIS:
This product has a WHMIS classification of E (corrosive material).

This product has been classified in accordance with the hazard criteria of the Controlled Products Regulations and this MSDS contains all of the information required by those regulations.

Canadian Ingredient Disclosure List:
CAS# 1310-73-2 is listed on the Canadian Ingredient Disclosure List.

CAS# 497-19-8 is listed on the Canadian Ingredient Disclosure List.

Section 16 - Additional Information
MSDS Creation Date: MAY/04/2006.

Most Recent Revision Date: MAY/01/2013.

Most Recent Revision: Version 5.

Addendum
Safety Precautions for Sodium Hydroxide:

http://www.certified-lye.com/safety.html

Protective Equipment for Use with Sodium Hydroxide:

http://www.certified-lye.com/protect.html

The information in this Material Safety Data Sheet for sodium hydroxide is believed to be accurate and represents the best information currently available to Certified Lye. However, Certified Lye makes no warranty of merchantability or any other warranty, express or implied, with respect to such information, and Certified Lye assumes no liability resulting from its use. Users should make their own investigations to determine the suitability of the information for their particular purposes. In no event shall Certified Lye be liable for any claims, losses, or damages of any third party or for lost profits or any special, indirect, incidental, consequential or exemplary damages, howsoever arising, even if Certified Lye has been advised of the possibility of such damages.

The information contained in the preceding MSDS is updated regularly. For an updated MSDS for sodium hydroxide, refer to http://www.certified-lye.com/MSDS-Lye.pdf.

Chapter 4
Choosing a Scale

Historically, a scale was a measuring device with a pointer and a spring. A balance was a lever with pans and the user placed standard weights on the pans to determine the resulting weight. Today, scales and balances are both digital. All soapmaking ingredients should be weighed for accuracy.

Steps to Choosing a Scale

1. How much do you want to weigh?

2. What will the maximum capacity be?

3. How accurate do you want to be? Is the scale accurate?

4. Why is accuracy important?

5. Which is a smaller unit of measure and therefore more accurate, 0.1 ounce or 1 gram?

6. For an electronic scale: Can the "auto-off" feature be disabled?

Capacity versus Readability

Capacity is the maximum weight a scale can register. Readability is the smallest increment the scale can register. For example, if the scale reads 10.1, then the readability is one tenth of an ounce.

    .1 = one tenth of an ounce
    .01 = one hundredth of an ounce
    .001 = one thousandth of an ounce

Capacity and readability are stated as "20 lb x 0.1 oz" (weighs up to 20 pounds at increments of one tenth of an ounce). Similarly, "200.00 g x 0.01 g" weighs up to 200 grams at increments of one hundredth of a gram.

    1.0 pound = 16.0000 ounces
    1.0 ounce = 28.3495 grams
    0.1 ounce =   2.8349 grams
    1.0 gram   =   0.0352 ounce
    0.1 gram   =   0.0035 ounce

Recommended Digital Scale

The Pelouze PS20 (pictured) has a capacity of 20 lbs and a readability of 0.1 ounce. It is available for about $45 from http://astore.amazon.com/soapstudio-20/detail/B00008IOX7

Chapter 5
Choosing a Soap Mold

Soap Molds

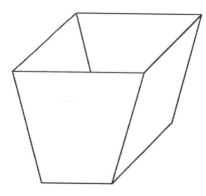

Choose a mold that will allow the soap to be removed easily; the opening of the mold should be slightly wider than the base or the mold should disassemble.

Soap molds may be made of any sturdy material, such as plastic, wood, heavy cardboard, or etc. Raw soap batter should not contact any metal other than stainless steel, so avoid wooden molds with metal fasteners, hinges, or bolts. Molds should be lined or coated for easier release of soap from the mold. Metal molds should be lined with a waterproof liner, such as a plastic trash bag. Wooden molds may be lined with a plastic liner, parchment paper, or silicone inserts. Plastic molds may be lined with inexpensive coatings of fat, such as Crisco, coconut, or palm oil.

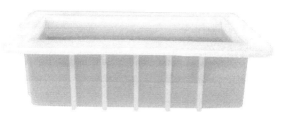

The class soap recipe is made using the Crafter's Choice silicone loaf mold #1501, available from the Soapmaking Studio or from http://www.soapmakingstudio.com/soapmaking-supplies/soap-molds.html. The flexible silicone allows for easy release of the finished soap loaf and the mold may be washed in a dishwasher.

Chapter 6
Creating the Soap Recipe

Soap Mold Capacity → Weight of Soap → Weight of Fats → Weight of Lye → Weight of Water

Determine the Soap Mold Capacity

Determine how much soap your mold will hold. The weights of water and of raw soap batter are not the same but they are very similar. Place the empty mold on the scale and tare the scale, so the weight of the mold itself will not be included in the final weight. Determine the weight of water the mold will hold by filling the mold with water and weighing it on the scale. When using a wooden mold, cut open a clean unused plastic kitchen trash bag (to obtain a thin sheet of plastic) and use it to line and protect the wooden mold before filling it with water. For this example, assume the water in the mold weighs 40 ounces.

↓

The Weight of Soap is Determined by the Soap Mold Capacity

If the soap mold has a capacity of 40 ounces of water, then create a soap recipe for 40 ounces of soap.

↓

The Weight of Fats (Oils) is Determined by the Weight of Soap (Pages 17 and 18)

The total weight of the fats should be 65% of the desired weight of the soap.
To make 40 ounces of soap, begin the soap recipe with 26 total ounces of fat because:
40 ounces of soap × 0.65 = 26 ounces of fat.

↓

The Weight of Lye is Determined by the Weight and Type of Fats (Page 24)

Use the saponification value from each oil's specification sheet to determine how much lye is needed to turn each oil into soap. The sum of the different weights of lye will total the quantity needed for the recipe, which should then be discounted (slightly reduced) (see page 25).
26 ounces of avocado oil × 0.1337 (Sap Value of avocado oil) = 3.4762 ounces of lye.
3.4762 ounces of lye discounted to 97% is 3.4762 × 0.97 = 3.3719 discounted ounces of lye.

↓

The Weight of the Water is Determined by the Weight of the Lye (Page 26)

After discounting the lye, used the discounted amount of lye to calculate the weight of the water for the soap recipe:
3.3719 discounted ounces of lye ÷ 0.3 = 11.2396 ounces of lye-water solution.
11.2396 ounces of lye-water solution − 3.3719 ounces of lye = 7.8677 ounces of water.

Calculate the Weight of the Fats

Always calculate the weight of the fats at 65% of the weight of the soap:
Weight of the soap × 0.65 = total weight of fats for the soap recipe.

Soapmaking Journal

Keep a soapmaking journal or recipe log of each batch of soap. Accurately record the weight or measurement of all ingredients to be able to adjust and improve the recipe each time it is made. In the back of the soapmaking journal, keep a record of all soap molds and their capacities.

1. Describe the class soap mold for later reference.

2. What is the soap mold capacity in ounces?

3. What is the weight of the soap to make during class? Remember, we do not want the soap mold filled to the brim; make 3 ounces less than the maximum capacity.

   Maximum mold capacity is _____ ounces.

   Weight of soap to make during class is _____ ounces.

4. What is the weight of the fats? Remember, the fats will be approximately 65% of the total weight of the soap.

5. Proportion the total weight of the fats among these three oils:

   20% coconut oil: _____ total ounces of fat × 0.20 = _____ ounces coconut oil.

   30% palm oil: _____ total ounces of fat × 0.30 = _____ ounces palm oil.

   50% olive oil: _____ total ounces of fat × 0.50 = _____ ounces olive oil.

6. Double-check the total of the percentages: 20% + 30% + 50% = 100%. Double-check the weights of the three oils, the total sum of all three oils should equal the total weight of the fats (as determined in step 4, above).

If 65% of the weight of the soap is fat, the remaining 35% is a combination of the lye, the water, and additives. Soap additives include essential oils, fragrance oils, herbs, colorant, or any ingredient that is not the actual soap. The average content of soap ingredients may vary greatly when using oils with extreme saponification values, such as coconut oil (which will require more lye) or jojoba oil (which will require less lye). Always measure ingredients by weight (ounces or grams), not by volume (cups or teaspoons). Use either ounces or grams but remain consistent throughout the calculations, do not switch back and forth.

1203 HALL AVENUE • RIVERSIDE3 • CALIFORNIA • 92509
T: 1(800) 988-OILS (951) 823-8490 • F: (951) 823-8491

Lot 5-18-22-05

AVOCADO OIL, REFINED
MATERIAL SPECIFICATIONS

PRODUCT DESCRIPTION: The fatty Avocado Oil is obtained by pure mechanical pressing from the fruit pulp of the ripe Avocado pear (Persea Americana. resp. Persea Gratissima). The pressed oil is of green to reddish-brown color. The subsequent refining considerably reduces the free fatty acids, and a light yellow, practically odorless oil is obtained. The cold filtration (winterization) can improve the cold stability (turbity) at certain temperatures. The main cultivation areas of the avocado tree are California, Mexico, south Africa and Israel. But today it is also grown in Central Afica and in South America.

PROPERTIES	TYPICAL ANALYSIS
Density at 20°C	0,912 - 0,923
Refractive Index at 20° C	1,468 - 1,476
Acid value	max. 1
Iodine value	80 - 95
Saponification value	187 - 195
Unsaponifable Matt	max. 2,0%

FATTY ACID COMPOSITION

Saturated fatty acid	C16:0	max.2%
Palmitic acid	C16:0	5 - 25%
Palmitoleic acid	C16:1	1 -12%
Stearic acid	C18:0	max.3%
Oleic	C18:1	50 - 74%
Linoleic acid	C18:2	6 -20%
Linolenic acid	C18:3	max. 3%
Other fatty acids		max. 1%

Shelf Life: 15 Months

Storage: Best strored in full containers, nitrogen blanketed, light protected and not above room temperature. Once open, to be stored at a cool place, nitrogen blanketed and to be used within 3 to 8 weeks, depending o the quality needed.

Usage: The unsaponifiable matter is composed of linear hydrocarbones, squalene, and phytoserols said to have cosmetic effects (e.g. great spreadability). Mild and skin softening, Avocado Oil is one of the major bases for many cosmetic skin and body care products (bath lotions, skin moistioners, creams, soaps etc.).

**DISTRIBUTORS AND
PROCESSORS OF
EXOTIC OILS**

Natural Oils International, Inc.
2279 Ward Ave
Simi Valley CA 93065
Phone: (805) 433-0160
Toll Free: 1-877-628-6457 (1-877-NATOILS)

Typical Specification: Avocado Oil, Expeller Pressed,
Refined, Bleached, Deodorized & Winterized
(Persea)
CAS: 8024-32-6
INCI: Persea americana

Additives		None
AOM Stability (hours),	(A.O.C.S. Cd 12-57)	--
Appearance		Clear Yellow
Cold Test (5 ½ Hrs. at 0° C.),	(A.O.C.S. Cc 11-53)	Pass
Color (5 ¼ Lovibond Scale),	(A.O.C.S. Cc 13b-45)	.6-1.4 R / 6-14 Y
Congealing Point/Titre °F.,	(A.O.C.S. Cc 14-59)	-5
FFA	(A.O.C.S. Ca 5a-40)	3 max.
Flavor Taste		Bland
Iodine Value (Wijs or Hanus),	(A.O.C.S. Cd 16-87)	65 - 95
Moisture %,	(A.O.C.S. Ca 2a-45)	.05 max.
Odor		Pleasant
Peroxide Value (at time of drumming),	(A.O.C.S. Cd 8-53)	<0.5
Refractive Index at 40° C.,	(A.O.C.S. Cc 7-25)	1.460 – 1.479
Saponification Value,	(A.O.C.S. Cd 3-25)	177 – 198
Smoke Point, °F.,	(A.O.C.S. Cc 9a-48)	520
Specific Gravity at 25° C.,	(A.O.C.S. Cc 10a-25)	0.908 – 0.920

FATTY ACID PROFILE · (A.O.C.S. Ce 5b-89)

Saturated: 16-22%	Monounsaturated: 66-72%	Polyunsaturated: 8-17%
C16: Palmitic 12-16%	C16:1 Palmitoleic 4.3-6.8%	C18:2 Linoleic 8-15%
C18: Stearic 2 max	C18:1 Oleic 60-72%	C18:3 Linolenic 2 max

Lot No: AVOC20091005

Chapter 8
Understanding Saponification Values

The potassium hydroxide (KOH) saponification value of avocado oil is 187.50 because it is the average of the saponification value range given on the Avocado Oil Specification Sheet from Natural Oils International, on page 20.

The KOH saponification range from the oil specification sheet is **177 – 198**.
To find the average, add the numbers and divide by two: (177 + 198) ÷ 2 = **187.50**.

Fat	KOH Sap Value	Use the Saponification Value to Calculate the Amount of Lye Needed		
		× 40 = 40 is the molecular weight of NaOH	÷ 56.1 = 56.1 is the molecular weight of KOH	÷ 1,000 = Amount of Lye Needed to Saponify 1 Unit of Fat
Almond Oil	191.76	191.76 × 40 = 7670.4	7670.4 ÷ 56.1 = 136.72	0.1367
Avocado Oil	(187.50)	187.50 × 40 = 7500.0	7500.0 ÷ 56.1 = 133.68	0.1337
Canola Oil	186.28	186.28 × 40 = 7451.2	7451.2 ÷ 56.1 = 132.82	0.1328
Castor Oil	180.36	180.36 × 40 = 7214.4	7214.4 ÷ 56.1 = 128.59	0.1286
Cocoa Butter	193.33	193.33 × 40 = 7733.2	7733.2 ÷ 56.1 = 137.84	0.1378
Coconut Oil	267.93	267.93 × 40 = 10717.2	10717.2 ÷ 56.1 = 191.03	0.1910
Corn Oil	191.89	191.89 × 40 = 7675.6	7675.6 ÷ 56.1 = 136.81	0.1368
Lard	196.26	196.26 × 40 = 7850.4	7850.4 ÷ 56.1 = 139.93	0.1399
Olive Oil	189.81	189.81 × 40 = 7592.4	7592.4 ÷ 56.1 = 135.33	0.1353
Palm Kernel Oil	249.26	249.26 × 40 = 9970.4	9970.4 ÷ 56.1 = 177.72	0.1777
Palm Oil	199.15	199.15 × 40 = 7966.0	7966.0 ÷ 56.1 = 141.99	0.1420
Peanut Oil	191.72	191.72 × 40 = 7668.8	7668.8 ÷ 56.1 = 136.69	0.1367
Safflower Oil	192.70	192.70 × 40 = 7708.0	7708.0 ÷ 56.1 = 137.39	0.1374
Sesame Oil	187.37	187.37 × 40 = 7494.8	7494.8 ÷ 56.1 = 133.59	0.1336
Soybean Oil	190.59	190.59 × 40 = 7623.6	7623.6 ÷ 56.1 = 135.89	0.1359
Sunflower Oil	190.45	190.45 × 40 =	÷ 56.1 =	0.1358
Tallow (Beef)	199.01	199.01 × 40 =	÷ 56.1 =	
Tallow (Mutton)	194.13	× 40 =		
Wheat Germ Oil	185.01			

KOH is potassium hydroxide, which is a larger molecule than NaOH, sodium hydroxide (lye). "Sap" is short for "saponification." Coconut oil and palm kernel oil require more lye to saponify, due to high lauric acid contents. Lard is pork fat. The vegetable alternative to lard is palm oil. Tallow is fat from either beef or mutton. Mutton refers to sheep.

Chapter 9
Chart of Saponification Values

Saponification Values for Making Soap with Lye (Sodium Hydroxide)	
Fat or Oil	**Lye (Sodium Hydroxide) NaOH**
♥ Indicates a fat not from an animal source. Animal! Indicates a fat from an animal source. These saponification values indicate the amount of lye (sodium hydroxide) needed to completely saponify the listed fat using consistent units of weight.	
Almond Oil ♥	0.1367
Aloe Vera Butter ♥	0.1788
Aloe Vera Oil ♥	0.1421
Apricot Kernel Oil ♥	0.1378
Avocado Butter ♥	0.1339
Avocado Oil ♥	0.1337
Babassu Nut Oil ♥	0.1749
Beeswax Animal!	0.0689
Borage Oil ♥	0.1339
Candelilla Wax ♥	0.0322
Canola Oil ♥	0.1328
Canola Oil, High Oleic Acid ♥	0.1330
Castor Bean Oil ♥	0.1286
Cherry Kernel Oil ♥	0.1389
Chicken Fat Animal!	0.1356
Cocoa Butter ♥	0.1378
Coconut Oil, Refined 76 °F ♥	0.1910
Coconut Oil, Hydrogenated 92 °F ♥	0.1910
Coconut Oil, Fractionated/Saturated ♥	0.2321
Copha® Vegetable Shortening ♥	0.1910
Corn Oil ♥	0.1368
Cottonseed Oil ♥	0.1387
Crisco® Vegetable Shortening ♥	0.1369
Emu Oil Animal!	0.1377
Evening Primrose Oil ♥	0.1362
Flaxseed Oil ♥	0.1358
Goat Fat Animal!	0.1382
Goose Fat Animal!	0.1349

Saponification Values for Making Soap with Lye (Sodium Hydroxide)	
Fat or Oil	**Lye (Sodium Hydroxide) NaOH**
Grapeseed Oil ♥	0.1321
Hazelnut Oil ♥	0.1369
Hempseed Oil ♥	0.1359
Jojoba Seed Oil ♥	0.0695
Jojoba Seed Liquid Wax ♥	0.0695
Karite Butter ♥	0.1296
Kremelta® Vegetable Shortening ♥	0.1910
Kukui Nut Oil ♥	0.1351
Lanolin Animal!	0.0748
Lard Animal!	0.1399
Linseed Oil ♥	0.1358
Macadamia Nut Oil ♥	0.1391
Milk Fat Animal!	0.1599
Mink Oil Animal!	0.1403
Monoï de Tahiti Oil ♥	0.1796
Neem Tree Oil ♥	0.1372
Olive Oil ♥	0.1353
Ostrich Oil Animal!	0.1385
Palm Kernel Oil ♥	0.1777
Palm Oil ♥	0.1420
Peach Kernel Oil ♥	0.1361
Peanut Oil ♥	0.1367
Pumpkin Seed Oil ♥	0.1389
Rapeseed Oil ♥	0.1328
Rice Bran Oil ♥	0.1284
Safflower Oil, High Linoleic Acid ♥	0.1374
Safflower Oil, High Oleic Acid ♥	0.1369
Sesame Seed Oil ♥	0.1336
Shea Butter ♥	0.1296
Soybean Oil ♥	0.1359
Soybean Oil, 27.5% Hydrogenated ♥	0.1361
Stearic Acid, Animal-Source Animal!	0.1413
Stearic Acid, Vegetable-Source ♥	0.1411
Sunflower Seed Oil ♥	0.1358

Saponification Values for Making Soap with Lye (Sodium Hydroxide)	
Fat or Oil	**Lye (Sodium Hydroxide) NaOH**
Sunflower Seed Oil, High Oleic Acid ♥	0.1351
Tallow, Beef Animal!	0.1419
Tallow, Deer Animal!	0.1382
Tallow, Sheep Animal!	0.1384
Tamanu Seed Oil ♥	0.1437
Tiaré Flower Oil ♥	0.1796
Walnut Oil ♥	0.1349
Wheat Germ Oil ♥	0.1319

0.1337 ounce of lye will completely saponify 1.0 ounce of avocado oil.
1.0 gram of avocado oil will be completely saponified by 0.1337 gram of lye.
1.0 pound of avocado oil will be completely saponified by 0.1337 pound of lye.
1.0 ton of avocado oil will be completely saponified by 0.1337 ton of lye.
10 ounces of avocado oil will be completely saponified by 1.337 ounces of lye.
100 ounces of avocado oil will be completely saponified by 13.37 ounces of lye.
1,000 ounces of avocado oil will be completely saponified by 133.7 ounces of lye.
26 ounces of avocado oil × 0.1337 (Sap Value of avocado oil) = 3.4762 ounces of lye.

Calculate the Weight of Lye for Each of the Oils in the Class Soap Recipe

4.8 ounces of coconut oil × 0.1910 (Sap Value of coconut oil) = _____ ounces lye.

7.2 ounces of palm oil × _____ (Sap Value of palm oil) = _____ ounces lye.

12.0 ounces of olive oil × _____ (Sap Value of olive oil) = _____ ounces lye.

Calculate the Weight of Lye for the Class Soap Recipe

Total weight of lye at 100% strength = _____ ounces of lye (add lye amounts).

Chapter 10
Lye Discount or Oil Superfat

If not enough lye is used to completely saponify all the fats, then some fats will freely remain unsaponified in the final bar of soap. It is a good idea to leave a small amount of free unsaponified fats so the soap will seem gentler and to account for any possible errors in measurements. In other words, it would be much better to have free oils in the soap than to have free lye in the soap. However, too many free oils in the soap will promote rancidity.

There are two different methods to calculate the amount of free oils to remain in the soap: "Lye discounting" and "oil superfatting."

Lye Discounting

Reducing (or discounting) the amount of lye so not all of the oils will saponify is termed "lye discounting." Instead of using 100% of the lye needed to saponify all of the oils, discount the lye to anywhere from 94% to 97%.

For example, to make 40 ounces of avocado oil soap:

The fats will be 65% of the total weight of the soap (see pages 17 and 18).
40 ounces of soap × 0.65 = 26 ounces of fat (avocado oil).
26 ounces of avocado oil × 0.1337 (sap value of avocado oil) = 3.4762 ounces of lye.
So, to completely saponify all 26 ounces of avocado oil, use 3.4762 ounces of lye.

To discount the 3.4762 ounces of lye to 97%:

3.4762 ounces of lye × 0.97 = 3.3719, or 3.3 ounces of lye. It is better to round down and have a bit less lye than to round up and have too much lye. Although it should be safe to use up to 3.4762 ounces of lye, which is the amount of lye at 100%.

Either discount the lye or superfat the oils; do NOT do both!

Oil Superfatting

To superfat a soap recipe, add more fat. Instead of using 100% of the fat, superfat the weight of the oil anywhere from 103% to 106% and use the weight of the lye at 100%.

To superfat the above example to 103%:

26 ounces of avocado oil superfatted to 103% is 26 × 1.03 = 26.78 ounces of avocado oil.
Use the lye from the above calculation at 100%, which is 3.4762 ounces of lye.

Lye Discount or Oil Superfat

If you discount the lye to less than 100%, then use the fats at 100%. If you superfat the oils to more than 100%, then use the lye at 100%. To keep from overfilling the mold by adding more oils, it is best to discount the weight of the lye.

Chapter 11
Calculating the Water

Measure Consistently by Weight, Not by Volume

Never measure ingredients by volume, such as by cups or tablespoons. Always measure ingredients by weight, such as by pounds, ounces, or grams. Be sure to use the same unit of measure for all ingredients. Consistently measure both the lye and the fats in ounces, or measure both the lye and the fats in grams. For example, avocado oil has a converted lye saponification value of 0.1337. So, it will require 0.1337 of an ounce of lye to saponify one ounce of avocado oil. Also, 0.1337 of a gram of lye is needed to saponify one gram of avocado oil. Likewise, 0.1337 of a pound of lye will saponify one pound of avocado oil.

Calculating and Measuring Water

Water is needed to dissolve the lye (sodium hydroxide) and for the hydrolysis of the fats. Using too much water may produce soft bars of soap, may demand extra drying time, or may encourage rancidity. Because the water is used to dissolve the lye, the amount of lye will determine the amount of water. To calculate the correct weight of water, first determine the discounted weight of lye (sodium hydroxide). Divide the discounted weight of lye by 0.3 and then subtract the discounted weight of lye from the result.

1. (Weight of Fat) × (Saponification Value of the Fat) = (Weight of Lye)
2. Discount the lye and use the discounted weight in further calculation.
3. (Discounted Weight of Lye) ÷ 0.3 = (Total Weight of Lye-Water Solution)
4. (Total Weight of Lye-Water Solution) − (Discounted Weight of Lye) = (Weight of Water)

For example, to make 26 ounces of avocado oil into soap:

1. Determine the Weight of the Lye
26 ounces of avocado oil × 0.1337 (Sap Value of avocado oil) = 3.4762 ounces of lye.

2. Discount the Lye
3.4762 ounces of lye discounted to 97% is 3.4762 ounces of lye × 0.97 = 3.3719 ounces of lye.

3. Discounted Weight of Lye ÷ 0.3 = Total Weight of Lye-Water Solution
3.3719 ounces of lye ÷ 0.3 = 11.2396 ounces of lye-water solution.

4. Total Weight of Lye-Water Solution − Discounted Weight of Lye = Weight of Water
11.2396 ounces of lye-water solution − 3.3719 ounces of lye = 7.8677 ounces of water.

Calculations and Decimals

For accuracy, carry all calculations to four decimals and continue to work through all equations with all four decimal places, even though the digital scale only displays one decimal place.

Water Quality

Tap, well, rain, and deionized water contain trace minerals and salts, which may promote discoloration and oxidation in soap. It is best to use distilled water.

Always add the lye to the water; never pour water on top of the lye!

Chapter 12
The Class Soap Recipe

The silicone loaf mold will easily hold 37 ounces of soap without overflowing.

Step 1: Determine the Total Weight of the Fats (Pages 17 and 18)

Our soap mold of 37 ounces will contain a soap recipe that is 65% fats.
37 ounces of soap × 0.65 = 24.05 ounces of fats but the scale can only display 24.0.

Step 2: Calculate the Weight of Each Fat

The class soap fat proportions are 20% coconut oil, 30% palm oil, and 50% olive oil.
Coconut oil will be 20% of the 24 ounces of fat: 0.20 × 24 = 4.8 ounces coconut oil.
Palm oil will be 30% of the 24 ounces of fats: 0.30 × 24 = 7.2 ounces palm oil.
Olive oil will be 50% of the 24 ounces of fats: 0.50 × 24 = 12.0 ounces olive oil.

Double-Check the Total Weight of the Fats
      4.8 ounces of coconut oil
      7.2 ounces of palm oil
 + 12.0 ounces of olive oil
     24.0 total ounces of fats

Step 3: Use the Chart of Saponification Values (Page 22) to Calculate the Lye

4.8 ounces coconut oil × 0.1910 (sap value of coconut oil) = _____ ounces lye.

7.2 ounces palm oil × _____ (sap value of palm oil) = _____ ounces lye.

12.0 ounces olive oil × _____ (sap value of olive oil) = _____ ounces lye.

Total weight of lye at 100% strength = _____ ounces of lye (add lye amounts).

Step 4: Discount the Lye to 96% (Page 25)

100% strength _____ ounces lye × 0.96 = _____ discounted ounces lye.

Step 5: Calculate the Weight of Water (Page 26)

_____ discounted ounces lye ÷ 0.3 = _____ ounces lye-water solution.

_____ oz lye-water solution – _____ discounted oz lye = _____ oz water.

Step 6: The Class Soap Recipe Totals

Lye		Water		Fat
_____ ounces lye	+	_____ ounces water	+	4.8 ounces coconut oil 7.2 ounces palm oil 12.0 ounces olive oil

= Soap

Chapter 13
Make Your Own Soap at Home

Don't be afraid to make your own soap at home. Soapmaking is a fun and rewarding hobby. Remember, do not be afraid of lye but give it your respect and exercise caution.

Keep notes and write down calculations in your soapmaking journal. Remember to record everything and precisely describe all calculations so you will be able to refer back to your work and understand it later.

Create the Soap Recipe

1. Choose a scale to measure your ingredients, such as lye, water, and fats. (Page 15.)

2. Find a suitable mold for your soap and describe the mold in your journal. (Pages 16 and 18.)

3. Zero out the weight of the mold from your scale (tare function) and weigh the mold filled with water to determine the maximum capacity of the mold and the weight of the soap. (Page 17.)

4. Calculate the total weight of the fats. (Page 18.)

5. Calculate the weight of each fat, based on the proportioning of recipe. (Page 18.)

6. Use the Chart of Saponification Values (page 22) to calculate the amount of lye needed for each individual fat and then add the individual amounts to determine the total amount of lye needed for the batch of soap. (Page 24.)

7. Discount the amount of lye. (Page 25.)

8. Calculate the amount of water. (Page 26.)

9. Review your final recipe and rewrite the amounts clearly in your journal as a formal recipe:
    a. Discounted weight of lye
    b. Weight of water
    c. Weight of each type of fat

Make the Soap

1. Allow yourself two hours' time to make your first batch of soap.

2. Have your work area and sink clean and free from clutter.

3. Assemble your scale, mold, safety glasses, apron, stainless steel pot, spoons, spatulas, stick blender, and other needed equipment.

4. Prepare the mold.

5. Weigh the water, then weigh the lye. Carefully add the lye to the water. This solution will now be termed "lye-water."

6. Weigh the solid fats and melt them.

7. Weigh the liquid fats and add them to the melted solid fats. Mix them together with a spatula or spoon. This mixture will now be termed "mixed fats."

8. Calculate the maximum amount of a skin-safe liquid scent material at the rate of 3% of the weight of the fats. For the soap recipe made in class, 24 total ounces of fats × 0.03 = 0.72 ounces of scent (maximum), which is almost equal to 4½ teaspoons. Add the liquid scent material to the "mixed fats" after the mixed fats have cooled to between 80 °F and 100 °F.

9. Measure ¼ to ½ teaspoon powdered pigment colorant, use more for a darker deep color or less for a lighter pastel color. Add the powdered pigment colorant to 1 tablespoon solution of soapy (distilled) water. This mixture will now be termed "wet colorant."

10. Carefully add the cooled lye-water to the mixed fats and stir/blend until the soap batter thickens to "trace." If layering or swirling the soap, separate the soap batter into portions.

11. Carefully add the wet colorant to the soap batter and thoroughly incorporate it until no variation in color is detectable. Short bursts with the blender will break up stubborn colorant.

12. Pour the soap batter into the mold.

13. Cover the mold with a lid or plastic wrap.

14. Insulate the filled mold well with towels, a blanket, or a heating pad.

The Final Bars of Soap

1. Remove the soap from the mold after at least 36 hours but not more than 72 hours.

2. Cut the soap into bars as soon as possible because the soap will be harder to cut when it has dried. Allow the bars to dry; wait a few days until most of the water has evaporated.

3. Examine the bars of soap. Look for any abnormalities and unevenness in color or texture. Write down a description of the final soap bars in your soapmaking journal.

4. Use a bar of the soap and write a description of the experience in your journal.

Notes

Bookstore

The Soapmaking Studio Bookstore is available online by clicking "Bookstore" from www.SoapmakingStudio.com or by visiting the bookstore directly: http://astore.amazon.com/soapstudio-20

Refer to this list of Bookstore categories because the Amazon format will not allow all possible category options to be viewed at the same time. Orders are fulfilled by Amazon.

Soapmaking Studio Bookstore

Soapmaking
>   Cold Process
>   >   Beginning
>   >   Intermediate
>   >   >   Milk Soap
>   >   Advanced
>   Hot Process
>   >   Liquid Soap
>   >   Transparent Bar Soap
>   >   Opaque Bar Soap
>   Melt and Pour
>   Rebatching

New Books

Magazines

Business
>   Start a Soap Business
>   Labeling and Packaging
>   Accounting
>   Business Entities

Chemistry

Fiction

Gardening

Miscellaneous
>   Appliances and Electronics
>   Essential Oils
>   Kindle Books
>   Unavailable

Libros en Español

SoapmakingStudio.com

Bookstore

Vendors

Soap Ingredients

Chemicals
>   Certified Lye ....http://www.certified-lye.com/

Fats (Base Oils and Butters)
>   Cibaria Soap Supply ....http://www.cibariasoapsupply.com/shop/
>   Natural Oils International ....http://www.naturaloils.com/
>   Soapmaking Studio ....http://www.soapmakingstudio.com/

Essential Oils
>   Liberty Natural Products ....http://www.libertynatural.com/
>   Soapmaking Studio ....http://www.soapmakingstudio.com/

Fragrance Oils
>   Soapmaking Studio ....http://www.soapmakingstudio.com/

Miscellaneous Supplies

Soap Molds
>   Ace Soap Molds ....http://www.acesoapmolds.com/
>   Golden Bright ....http://gbcraft.com/shop/silicone-mold
>   Soapmaking Studio ....http://www.soapmakingstudio.com/

Protective Equipment
>   Certified Lye...http://www.certified-lye.com/

Scales
>   Soapmaking Studio Bookstore (Misc.).....http://astore.amazon.com/soapstudio-20

Stick Blender or Wand Blender
>   Soapmaking Studio Bookstore (Misc.).....http://astore.amazon.com/soapstudio-20
>   Walmart ....http://www.walmart.com/

Information and Marketing

Advertising
>   Natural Soap Directory ....http://www.natural-soap-directory.com/

Articles
>   Pallas Athene Soap.......http://www.pallasathenesoap.com/home.html#MakeSoap

Books
>   Online Bookstore http://astore.amazon.com/soapstudio-20
>   In Stock ....http://www.soapmakingstudio.com/soapmaking-supplies/books.html

Groups and News
>   Facebook Group ....https://www.facebook.com/groups/soapmakingstudio/
>   Natural Soap News ....http://www.natural-soap-directory.com/soap-list.htm
>   SoCal Soapmakers' Luncheons .http://www.pallasathenesoap.com/luncheon.html

Soapmaking Studio
Registration Form

Student's Name: _____

Mailing Address: _____

City, State ZIP: _____

Telephone: _____

Email: _____

Registration for enrollment in the following class:

☐ Soapmaking 101, Beginning Cold Process Soapmaking

☐ Soapmaking 105, Intermediate Hot Process Soapmaking

☐ Soapmaking 210, Advanced Cold/Hot Process Soapmaking

☐ Soapmaking 214, Intermediate Transparent Bar Soapmaking

☐ Soapmaking 215, Intermediate Liquid Soapmaking

☐ Soapmaking 220, Coloring and Scenting Soap

☐ Soap Garden 224, Cultivating, Drying, and Adding Herbs to Soap

☐ Soapmaking 225, Water Substitution in Soapmaking

☐ Soap Business 320, Forming a Legal Business Entity to Sell Soap

☐ Soap Business 330, Soap Labeling and Marketing

☐ Soap Business 335, Shrink Wrapping Soap

☐ Soap Business 340, Packaging and Shipping Soap Worldwide

☐ Soap Business 350, Website Design and Internet Commerce

☐ Other class, such as a workshop or limited edition class:_____

Class information:

Class Date: _____

Class Time: _____

Instructor: _____

Class Fee: _____

Materials Fee: _____

Total Enrollment Fee: _____

Make check or money order payable to the Soapmaking Studio and mail to:

Soapmaking Studio
7301 Mount Vernon St
Lemon Grove, CA 91945-3122

Before mailing, make a copy of your completed registration form for your records.
Contact the Soapmaking Studio with any questions: (619) 245-8898 • info@SoapmakingStudio.com

Glossary

capacity. The maximum amount that can be contained.

cure. To process for storage or use. Before knowledge of formulations to complete the saponification process in the mold, soapmakers used to shelve soap on racks for six weeks to wait for the sodium hydroxide to pair with fatty acid molecules and form soap. The time spent waiting for the saponification reaction to complete so the soap could safely be used was termed "curing."

deliquesce. Melt, dissolve. A granule of sodium hydroxide left on a countertop will first appear as a grain of salt. After a few minutes, it will appear as a drop of liquid because sodium hydroxide will readily absorb moisture from the air and deliquesce.

deliquescent salt. Sodium hydroxide is a deliquescent salt; it will completely melt or dissolve if left open to the air.

desiccant. A usually small packet of silica gel intended to dry or dehydrate textiles and dry goods. Never store a desiccant packet inside a container of sodium hydroxide.

exothermic. Characterized by evolution of heat. Giving off heat. As sodium hydroxide dissolves in water and bonds are broken, energy is released in the form of heat. Upon adding sodium hydroxide to water, the solution will become very hot.

hygroscopic. Readily taking up and retaining moisture. Sodium hydroxide is hygroscopic; it will absorb moisture from the air.

insulate. To cover or wrap with material for the purpose of retaining heat. In cold process soapmaking, after the raw soap batter is poured into the mold, they are covered with a blanket or towel to keep the soap warm and to prevent rapid cooling.

lye. In this workbook, the term "lye" only refers to dry sodium hydroxide. When referencing a solution of sodium hydroxide dissolved in water, this workbook uses the term "lye-water." In most outside sources, the term "lye" may refer to either dry sodium hydroxide or a solution of sodium hydroxide dissolved in water.

lye discount. A deduction of the amount of sodium hydroxide needed for a soap recipe. After calculating the weight of sodium hydroxide necessary to turn the oils into soap, reduce the sodium hydroxide to 94–97%.

lye-water. A caustic liquid solution sodium hydroxide dissolved in water.

MSDS (Material Safety Data Sheet). A collection of safety information related to a specific compound. Intended to aid first responders and emergency personnel by defining procedures for working with, handling, or cleaning up spills of specific substances in a safe manner. Material Safety Data Sheets include the physical characteristics of a substance, first aid measures, recommended protective equipment, and test results.

oil specification sheet. A page of laboratory test results regarding a specific oil. Results include the saponification value of the oil, the iodine and peroxide values, and the fatty acid profile of the oil. The values of an oil specification sheet change with each lot number produced, even for the same type of oil.

potassium hydroxide. KOH. A corrosive chemical necessary for liquid soap manufacture. While potassium hydroxide occurs naturally in hardwood ashes, synthetically produced potassium hydroxide is readily available and is better quality. Oil specification sheets refer to the saponification value of potassium hydroxide.

readability. The smallest increment a scale can register. For example, a scale displaying a weight of 9.4 ounces has a readability of 0.1 ounce or one tenth of an ounce.

saponification completion. The occurrence of the end of the reaction between the lye, water, and oils to form soap. After the moment the reaction to form soap has been ended. Saponification completion was previously achieved by curing soap for six weeks (time) or by cooking the soap (heat). Saponification completion for cold process soap now occurs in the mold due to specific formulation (water).

saponification value. The number of milligrams of lye (sodium hydroxide) required to completely saponify one gram of a specific fat. Laboratories and oil specification sheets refer to the saponification value of potassium hydroxide, not sodium hydroxide.

saponify. To convert (a fat) into soap. To form soap. To become soap.

scent material. Cold process soap is easily scented with liquid scent materials, such as essential oils (plant extracts) or fragrance oils (synthetic). All scent materials must first be verified skin safe before use. Most scent materials are highly volatile; they have low flash point temperatures, are very flammable, and evaporate quickly. It is generally considered safe to add scent materials at the rate of 3% of the fats. Some scent materials will cause the raw soap batter to thicken very quickly.

silicone. An abundant, organic, non-metallic chemical compound. Soap molds made of silicone are prized for their ease of use. Silicone molds resist temperatures up to 500 °F, are dishwasher safe, and do not require liners.

soapmaking journal. Soapmakers should keep a journal or recipe log detailing the exact weight of all ingredients used in each batch of soap, a description of the soapmaking procedures (including times and temperatures), and comments about the final soap bars and any needed recipe modifications.

sodium hydroxide. NaOH. A corrosive chemical necessary for soap manufacture. While sodium hydroxide occurs naturally in hardwood ashes, synthetically produced sodium hydroxide is readily available and is better quality. Oil specification sheets refer to the saponification value of potassium hydroxide and the value must be converted to sodium hydroxide when making bar soap.

solvation. Dissolution. The action or process of dissolving. For example, the solvation of sodium hydroxide in water.

superfat. Adding more fat (or oils). Increasing the amount of fat in a soap recipe.

tare. A deduction from the gross weight of a substance and its container made in allowance for the weight of the container. Digital scales usually have a tare feature or special tare button to allow the weight display to be reset to null (zero) while a container or soap mold is on the scale. By using the tare feature, the weight displayed by the scale will not include the weight of the container.

trace. A measure of the thickness of raw soap batter. If a portion of raw soap batter is scooped up and dribbled back onto the surface of the soap batter and a trace of the dribbled soap remains slightly suspended on top of or above the surface and does not immediately sink back into the mass of soap batter, then trace has been achieved. Soapmakers used to patiently watch for the "trace" degree of thickness because if the soap was thick enough to support itself, then it was thick enough to support (and evenly suspend) additives.

unsaponified. Not made into soap. For example, excess fat may remain unsaponified in a bar of soap, so there will be oil molecules trapped within the soap.

Index

deliquescent, 4

exothermic, 2, 3

eye protection, 5, 7

hygroscopic, 4, 9

fat proportions, 18, 27, 28

insulate, 29

lye. *See* sodium hydroxide

MSDS (Material Safety Data Sheet), 3, 4, 8. *See also under* sodium hydroxide

oil specification sheet, 19, 20, 21

potassium hydroxide, 2, 21

recipe, 16, 17, 18, 24, 25

safety glasses, 5, 10

saponification, 2, 21

saponification value, 2, 17, 18, 21, 22, 25–28

saponify, 2, 21, 22, 24–26

scale, 15, 17, 26, 28, 29
    capacity, 15, 17, 18, 28
    readability, 15
    recommended digital scale, 15

scent material, 29

soapmaking journal, 18, 28, 29

soap mold, 16–18

sodium hydroxide
    discount, 25, 26
    first aid, 3
    quality, 4
    Material Safety Data Sheet, 9–14
    soap, 2
    storage, 4

superfat, 25

tare, 17, 28

trace, 26, 29

unsaponified, 25

vinegar, 3

water
    calculation, 17, 26, 27
    distilled, 26, 29

weight
    of fat, 17, 18, 26
    of lye, 17, 24, 26–28
    of water, 17, 26, 27

Made in the USA
Lexington, KY
26 December 2013